ALWAYS LOOKING UP

NANCY GRACE ROMAN, ASTRONOMER

LAURA GEHL

ILLUSTRATED BY
LOUISE PIGOTT
AND ALEX OXTON

Young Nancy Grace loved to look up at the endless night sky.
She gazed at tiny blue-white stars glittering in inky blackness.

Her father's job changed again and again. For Nancy Grace, this meant moving from Tennessee to Texas, to Oklahoma, to New Jersey, then to Michigan. Each new place seemed different and strange.

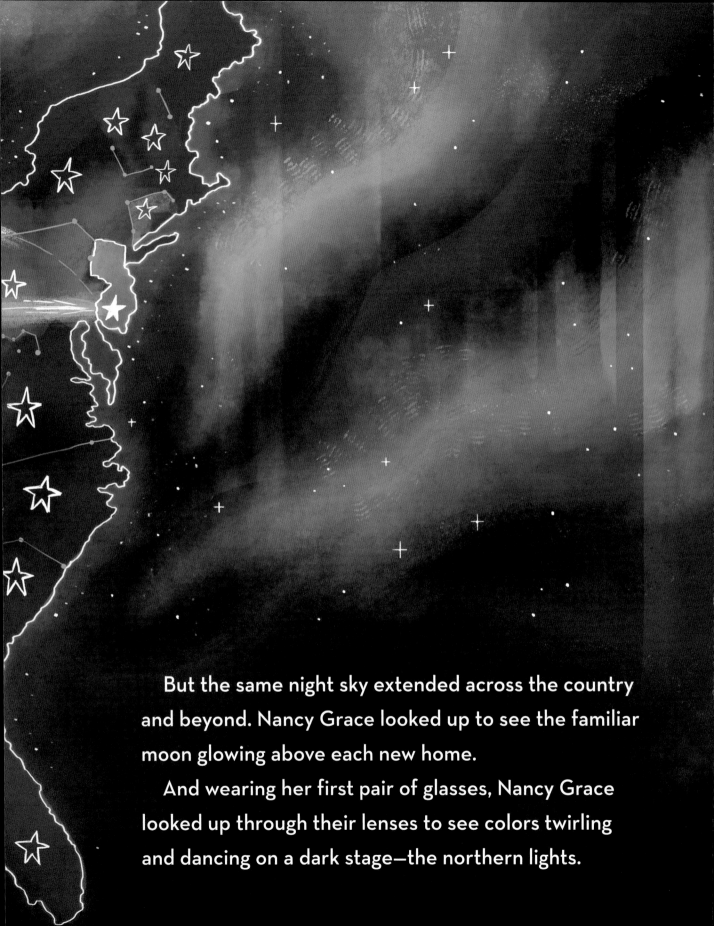

But the same night sky extended across the country and beyond. Nancy Grace looked up to see the familiar moon glowing above each new home.

And wearing her first pair of glasses, Nancy Grace looked up through their lenses to see colors twirling and dancing on a dark stage—the northern lights.

With curiosity as boundless as the universe, Nancy Grace vowed to learn more about space.

She gathered friends into an astronomy club to study the constellations. Together they mapped sparkling patterns on an infinite black canvas.

Standing in the quiet night, Nancy Grace watched
brilliant meteors shoot across an ocean of deep dark blue.
And she noticed Venus and Jupiter, outshining the stars.

1,000 A.D

0.A.D

1,000 B.C.

2,000 B.C.

α
3,000 B.C.

4,000 B.C.

5,000 B.C

20,000 A.D

19,000

18,000

17,000

3,000•Pole Star

2,000

4,000

5,000

β

ε

ζ

γ

Ursa Minor

η

χ

δ

Pole of the

ζ

η

Draco

Pole of the
Ecliptic

ε

δ

ι

β

ζ

ν

β

γ

τ

σ

Cepheus

β

π

α

cules

Nancy Grace read every astronomy book in the public library.

But then her eyes grew weak, and the doctor ordered a break: no reading except for schoolwork.

Still, no one could stop Nancy Grace from reading the night sky.

And she was unstoppable at school, where she tutored a fellow student in math, asked questions her physics teacher could not answer, and requested a second algebra class instead of Latin.

"What *lady* would take mathematics instead of Latin?" the guidance counselor asked.

A lady planning to be an astronomer, that's who!

With determination as fiery as a supernova, Nancy Grace went on to college, where her professors told her science and math were masculine subjects. Cold hard facts and calculations were best left to men, they believed. Literature and history, those were for women.

Yet Nancy Grace knew astronomy was for her.

Curving text around the spiral:

magnetic field far stron... If this is the true origin of the radiation of the ...tars, the sun is destroying its atoms at the rate or a re-arrangement of atoms. More probably in ...supernovas have enormous brilliat... the luminosity of a star has been determined ...all measurements must be made at great distance

And her eyes were strong again—strong enough to read a tower of books stretching toward space.

Nancy Grace blazed through science classes until one teacher admitted, "Maybe you just might make it."

Nancy Grace zoomed ahead to graduate school.
Some teachers did not approve of women pursuing
advanced degrees. They thought women should leave
school and get married instead.

But Nancy Grace stayed focused on the stars of the Big Dipper, studying their movements through space.

She still looked up at the sky every night—but now it was her job. Nancy Grace had pushed past everyone steering her toward "ladylike" careers, such as teaching or nursing. She had achieved her goal of becoming an astronomer.

Yet this was only the beginning.

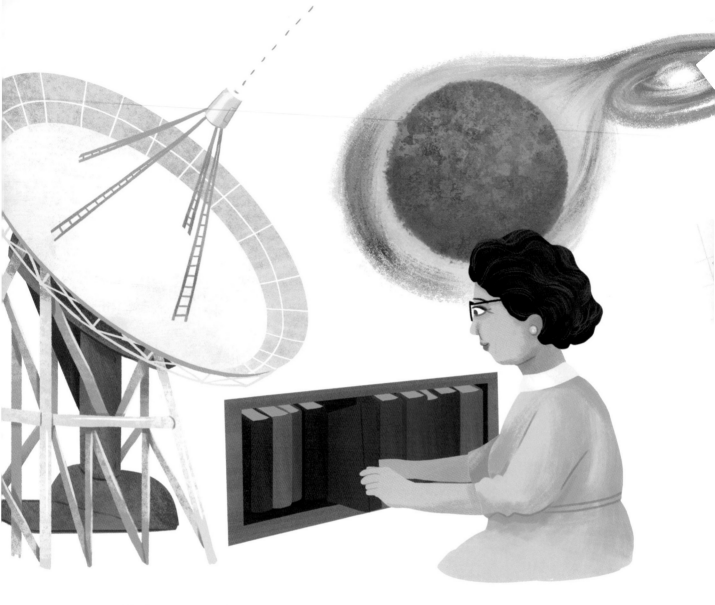

With powerful tools and her powerful mind, astronomer Nancy Grace searched for new information, new answers, even new questions about the universe.

She studied bright stars in our swirly Milky Way, noting that young stars moved differently from older ones.

She observed binary stars, like AG Draconis—a giant star and a dwarf star orbiting each other.

She worked with radio telescopes, detecting invisible energy from stars and planets.

Her research spread across the world to astronomers in the Soviet Union—where Americans were not normally welcome. They read Nancy Grace's published paper about AG Draconis and invited her to visit.

Nancy Grace's trip intrigued other scientists. She gave a talk when she returned to the US, then a series of ten astronomy lectures.

Nancy Grace's passion shone as she spoke. She had seen and learned so much in her career already. Now she could share that knowledge with others.

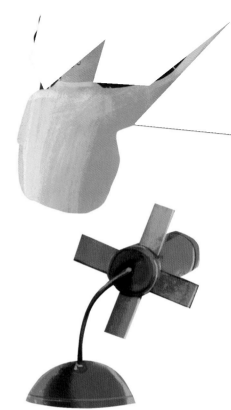

When brand-new NASA needed a chief of astronomy, Nancy Grace seized the opportunity.

She traveled the country, asking scientists about their hopes for space astronomy. Many had the same desire: a clear view of space from above the atmosphere. Nancy Grace understood that the atmosphere blocks and alters light from space. "Looking at stars through the atmosphere," she wrote in an essay, "is not too different from looking at streetlights through a pane of old stained glass."

Nancy Grace dreamed of helping astronomers see farther into space than humans had ever seen before— past the moon, past Venus and Jupiter, past the stars she had mapped as a child.

The world needed a new kind of telescope: one that floated above the atmosphere, orbiting Earth while capturing images of infant stars, black holes, and galaxies billions of light-years away.

Astronomers had wished for this type of telescope before, yet many doubted it could become a reality. A large space telescope would cost millions, maybe billions of dollars. It would be difficult to build. Telescopes on Earth were good enough.

But Nancy Grace had faced doubters before.

She brought astronomers and engineers together. What did astronomers want? What did engineers believe possible? What if something went wrong up in space? Meetings continued for years. Gradually, they agreed on a design. A design that would become the Hubble Space Telescope.

NASA needed money from Congress to pay for Hubble—lots of money. One senator questioned whether taxpayers should fund an expensive telescope. But Nancy Grace had experience defending her choices.

"For the price of a single night at the movies, every American...will get fifteen years of exciting scientific results," she wrote in response.

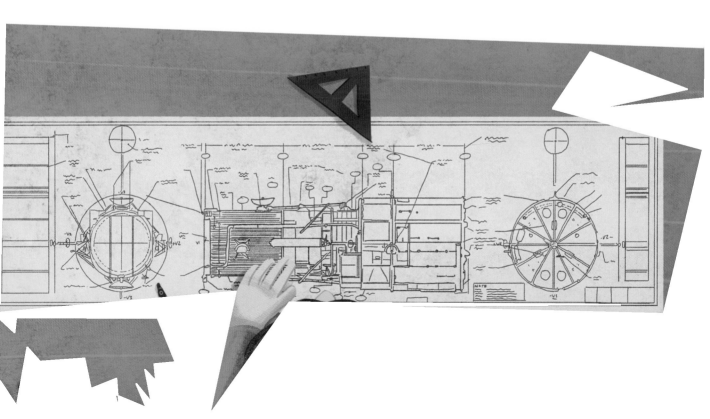

Finally, more than a decade later—following design changes, delays, and setbacks—a shuttle carried Hubble into space. As big as a bus, as heavy as two elephants, Hubble was launched into orbit.

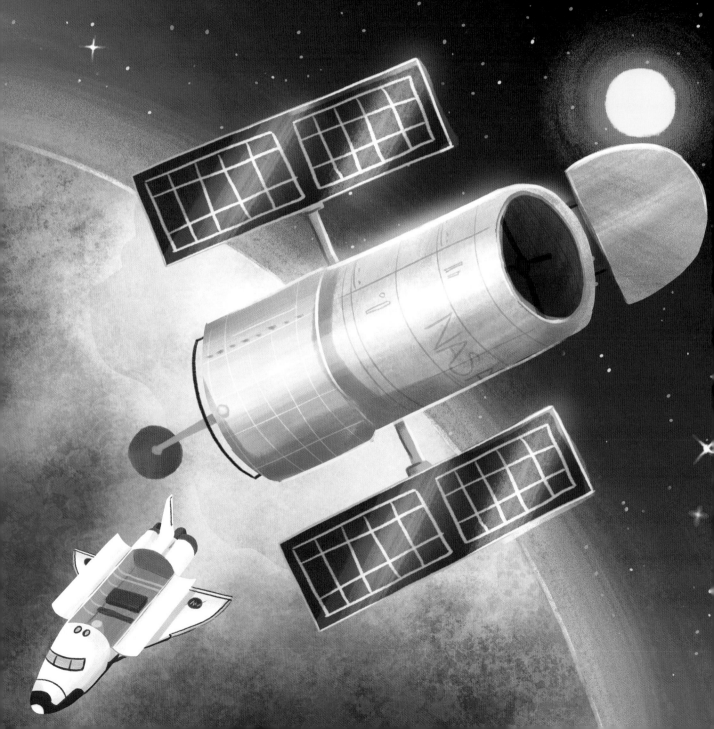

The world waited for the first photographs taken without the distortion of the atmosphere. Photographs that would prove Hubble worthy of the money and years of effort.

But the first images were blurry. And hopes plummeted like a falling meteorite.

Yet, way back when Nancy Grace brought a team together to design Hubble, they had repair missions in mind. Hubble was the first telescope designed to be serviced in space.

Three years after Hubble's launch, astronauts installed a device to correct the faulty mirror. It was like putting "glasses" on Hubble.

Once again, people across the globe waited for pictures. Would the fix work? Nancy Grace waited too.

Yes!

Crystal clear images from Hubble dazzled and delighted, informed and inspired.

Nancy Grace, called "Mother of Hubble," marveled along with the rest of the world at the photographs sent back from space—comets hurtling into Jupiter; dust storms on Mars; nebulae shaped like a butterfly, a crab, a tarantula.

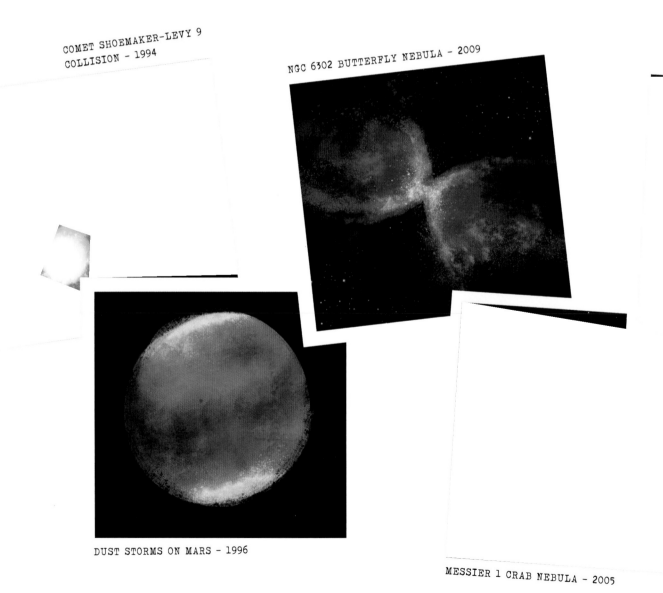

COMET SHOEMAKER-LEVY 9 COLLISION - 1994

NGC 6302 BUTTERFLY NEBULA - 2009

DUST STORMS ON MARS - 1996

MESSIER 1 CRAB NEBULA - 2005

Over the next quarter of a century—much longer than the fifteen years Nancy Grace had promised Congress—Hubble changed the way people saw the universe, and helped scientists make giant leaps in understanding space. Astronomers could track the shrinking red spot on Jupiter, measure the atmosphere of planets beyond our solar system, and estimate the age of the universe.

NGC 2060
TARANTULA NEBULA - 2011

JUPITER'S GREAT RED SPOT
AND GANYMEDE'S SHADOW - 2014

NGC 922 - 2012

IC 63 GHOST NEBULA - 2018

After retiring, Nancy Grace never stopped learning about astronomy—reading papers, attending lectures, talking with other astronomers. And even in her nineties, Nancy Grace loved to walk outside and look up at the endless night sky. As she said, "The real way to learn about the sky is to look at it."

Till rising and gliding out I wander'd off by myself,

In the mystical moist night-air, and from time to time,

Look'd up in perfect silence at the stars.

—Walt Whitman, from "When I Heard the Learn'd Astronomer,"
Nancy Grace Roman's favorite poem

AUTHOR'S NOTE

Many people over many decades worked to make the Hubble Space Telescope a reality. But only Nancy Grace earned the nickname "Mother of Hubble." Nancy Grace Roman, who struggled with weak eyesight as a child, helped astronomers—and everyone else on Earth—see farther into space than ever before.

While Nancy Grace is most famous as the "Mother of Hubble," her proudest accomplishment was launching a much smaller telescope into orbit. This telescope, called the International Ultraviolet Explorer (IUE), didn't take pictures. Nobody outside of the astronomy community knew or cared about its launch in 1978. But the IUE gave astronomers information about the wavelengths of ultraviolet light from objects in space. Scientists couldn't get that data from a ground-based telescope, because Earth's ozone layer blocks the UV wavelengths. Nancy Grace fought for this little satellite just like she fought for giant Hubble. And thanks to Nancy Grace, scientists have published more than five thousand research papers using data from the IUE.

While Nancy Grace was lucky her childhood problems with weak eyesight did not persist into adulthood, she never forgot those years when she wasn't allowed to read. After her retirement, Nancy Grace read astronomy books aloud for adults with dyslexia and impaired vision.

Nancy Grace also enjoyed talking with students and offered advice to kids who love science:

1. If you are a girl or a boy who wants to be a scientist, go for it!
2. Be flexible. Your career may lead you in unexpected directions.
3. Science is changing all the time, which means the right job for you might not even exist yet.

TIMELINE

1925 Nancy Grace Roman is born in Nashville, Tennessee.

1929 Edwin Hubble formulates Hubble's Law, leading to acceptance of the idea that the universe is expanding.

1935 Between fifth and sixth grade, Nancy Grace organizes her friends into an astronomy club.

1937 Seventh-grader Nancy Grace, having read every astronomy book in the public library, decides she will be an astronomer.

1946 Nancy Grace graduates from Swarthmore College with a BA in astronomy.

1949 Nancy Grace receives her PhD in astronomy from the University of Chicago. She continues her teaching and research at the University of Chicago until 1955.

1955 Nancy Grace takes a job in radio astronomy at the US Naval Research Laboratory.

1957 The Soviet Union launches Sputnik I, the first human-made Earth-orbiting satellite, igniting the space race between the Soviet Union and the United States.

1958 The United States creates the National Aeronautics and Space Administration (NASA).

1959 Nancy Grace joins NASA at its headquarters to develop a program in space astronomy. Her title will become Chief of Astronomy and Relativity Programs.

1961 Yuri Gagarin, Soviet cosmonaut, becomes the first person in space. Alan Shepard Jr. becomes the first American astronaut in space shortly afterward.

1969 Neil Armstrong becomes the first person to walk on the moon. Nancy Grace receives the NASA Exceptional Scientific Achievement Medal.

1977 Congress approves funding for the Hubble Space Telescope, in large part due to Nancy Grace's efforts.

1978 Nancy Grace receives the NASA Outstanding Leadership Medal.

1979 Nancy Grace retires from NASA to take care of her mother. She continues working on the Hubble Space Telescope and other astronomical projects as a consultant.

1983 Sally Ride becomes the first female American astronaut in space. NASA flies Nancy Grace to Florida for the launch.

1986 An asteroid is named 2516 Roman, after Nancy Grace. The space shuttle *Challenger* disaster delays Hubble's launch by several years.

1990 The Hubble Space Telescope is put into orbit. Blurry images transmitted back to Earth reveal a problem with the telescope's mirror.

1993 Astronauts repair Hubble in a series of space walks. Hubble begins to send crystal clear photographs back to Earth.

1995 Nancy Grace becomes director of the Astronomical Data Center at NASA's Goddard Space Flight Center.

1997 Nancy Grace retires for the second time.

2011 NASA establishes the Nancy Grace Roman Technology Fellowship in Astrophysics.

2018 Nancy Grace Roman passes away at the age of 93.

ACKNOWLEDGMENTS

I would like to thank the astronomers, experts, and friends who read drafts of this work, including Dr. Meg Urry, Dr. Margaret Weitekamp, Alan Ladwig, Meg Thacher, Dr. Edward J. Weiler, Dr. Charles Resnick, Jenna Resnick, Stacy McAnulty, Peter McCleery, Anthony Piraino, Deborah Beauchamp, Camille Andros, Jason Gallaher, Lori Richmond, Ann McCallum Staats, Hena Khan, and Joan Waites. Your help and encouragement were invaluable.

My husband, Ryan, and my children, Kevin, Nathan, Seth, and Tessa, support my work every day in many ways: thank you, and I love you.

Huge thanks also go to Stephen Garber, who first suggested I write this story; to my agent, Erzsi Deàk, who always believed in it; and to my editor, Wendy McClure, whose vision and insight made book the best it could be. Louise Pigott and Alex Oxton, working with designers Morgan Beck and Aphee Messer, brought the words to life so beautifully that I was moved to tears.

Most of all, I am grateful to Dr. Nancy Grace Roman, who invited me into her home, answered all of my questions, and generously shared her recollections, photographs, and mementos.

Library of Congress Cataloging-in-Publication data is on file with the publisher.

Text copyright © 2019 by Laura Gehl
Illustrations copyright © 2019 by Albert Whitman & Company
Illustrations by Louise Pigott and Alex Oxton
First published in the United States of America
in 2019 by Albert Whitman & Company
ISBN 978-0-8075-0296-9 (hardcover)
ISBN 978-0-8075-0297-6 (ebook)